Dear Maxwell

A Conversation About Race

words by

Tara Paige Hewan

Pictures by

Daniela Aguero

Towards Justice Publishing, LLC • Leesburg, VA 20176

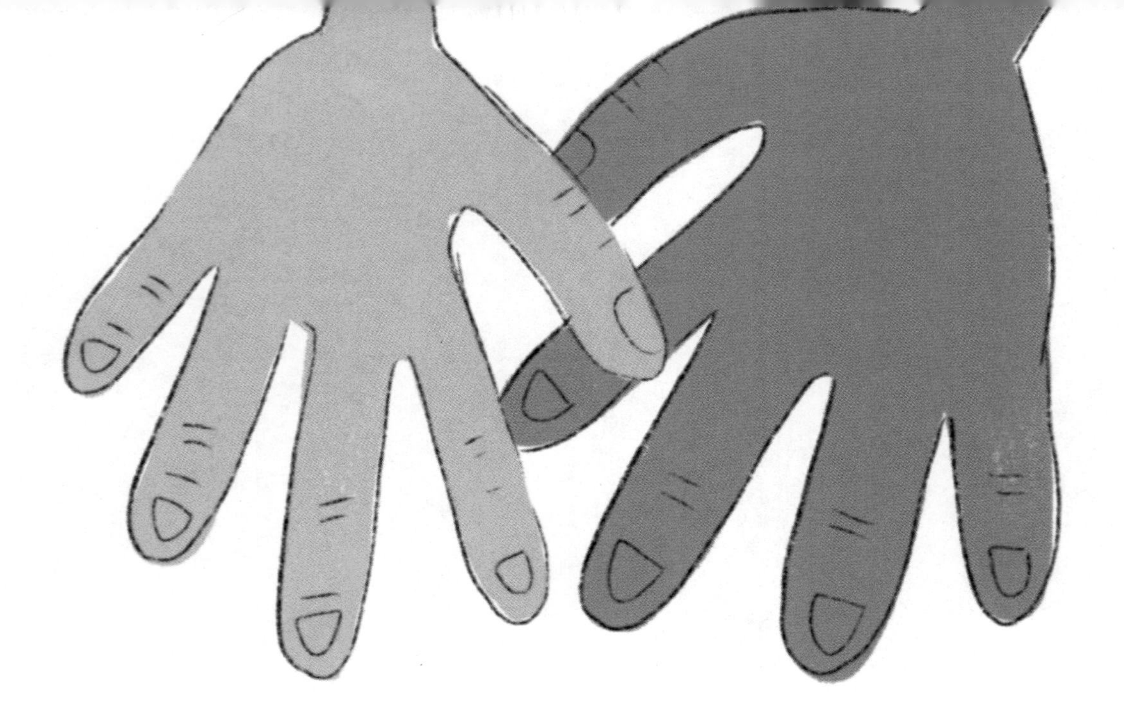

Printed in the United States

ISBN 978-1-7374369-0-4

Dear Maxwell is available in bulk at discount prices.
Learn more at liberationandjustice.com

This book is dedicated to my son Maxwell,
my daughter Imari and all the young
Black children who have ever had clouds
of inferiority form in their mental sky.
I see you. I love you. You matter.

To my husband, George and all my
family and friends who stand with me
in the fight towards justice.

Dear Maxwell,

you are made

wonderfully!

I am wonderfully made.

Dear Maxwell,

In my eyes you are made

PERFECT.

I hope you meet a lot of conscious people that will **see you as I do.**

Dear Maxwell,

Many people are waking up and understanding how **race impacts our lives.**

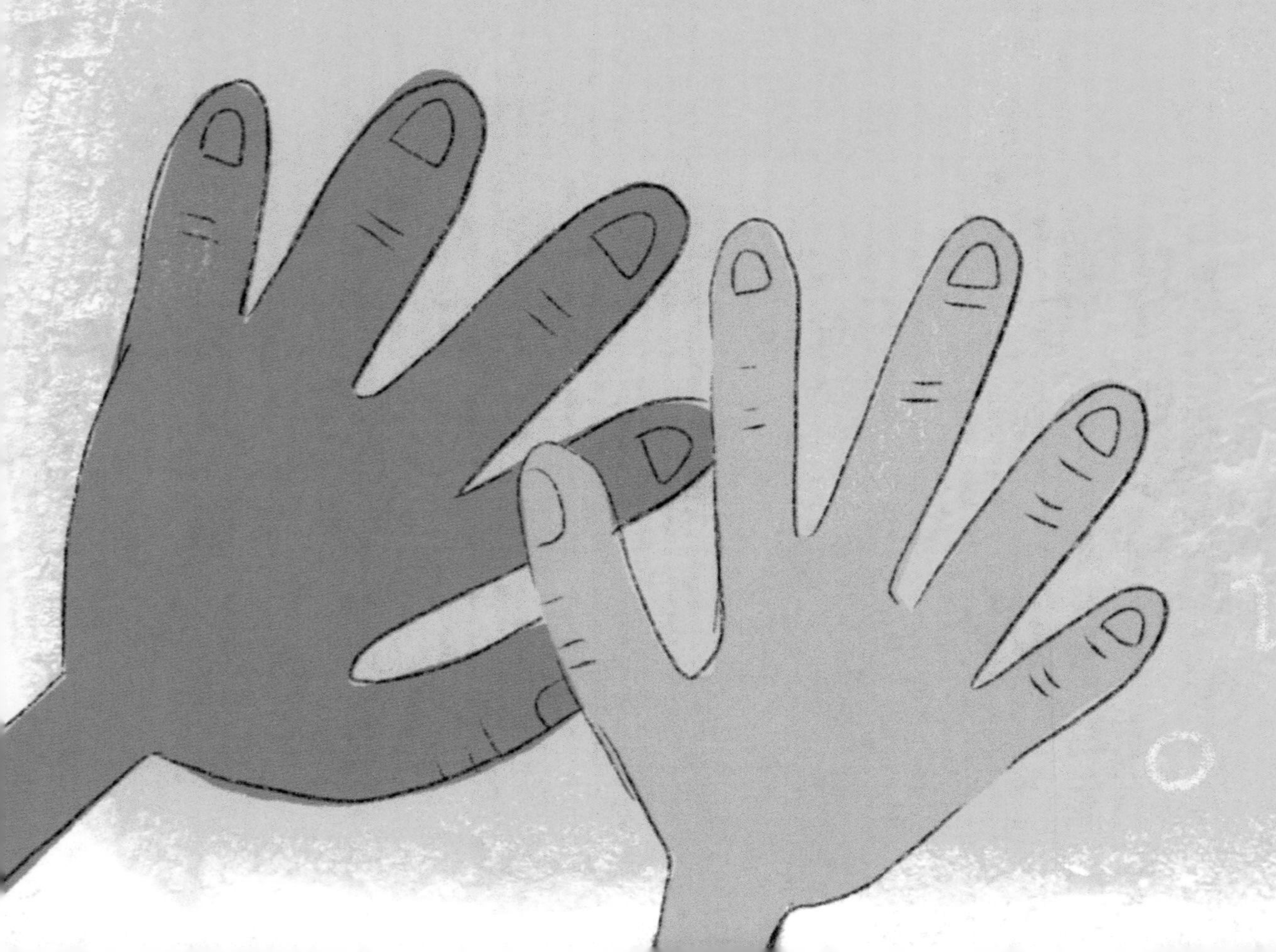

RACE?

Dear Maxwell,

Race is a social construct
that describes a **group of people.**

Dear Maxwell,

There are many different races and they are

ALL **EQUAL.**

Dear Maxwell,

your race is

Black

or

African American

Dear Maxwell,

you must **remember** that

ALL RACES ARE EQUAL

even when they are not treated the same way.

Dear Maxwell,

There are **rules, practices,** and **policies** that lead to unfair outcomes for some races.

VOTE

PROTECT
MY
VOTE

Dear Maxwell,

People get **hurt** by these rules.

Dear Maxwell,

These rules are **racist** and they

NEED TO CHANGE

Dear Maxwell,

We can change them.

We can abolish those rules.

OLD RULES
NEW RULES!

Dear Maxwell,

Many brave **women** and **men** have changed these rules.

Dear Maxwell,

Some people are hurting
because the rules make them
think they are **superior.**

Dear Maxwell,

Some people are hurting
because the rules make them
think they are **inferior.**

Dear Maxwell,

We can

change the rules.

We can

change the outcomes.

We can

help the people who are hurting.

BLACK
LIVES
MATTER
BLM

Dear Maxwell,

So that you can live in a world...

where you are

FREE

to be young

make mistakes

be silly

have fun

know joy!

Dear Maxwell,

Because...

you are made

WONDERFULLY!

Even when you don't do things that are wonderful.

Dear Maxwell,

you are made

wonderfully!

I am wonderfully made.

Made in the USA
Middletown, DE
25 July 2021